WHAT IS THE LEGISLATIVE BRANCH?

MATTHEW CUMMINGS

Britannica®
Educational Publishing

IN ASSOCIATION WITH

ROSEN
EDUCATIONAL SERVICES

Published in 2016 by Britannica Educational Publishing (a trademark of Encyclopædia Britannica, Inc.) in association with The Rosen Publishing Group, Inc.
29 East 21st Street, New York, NY 10010

Distributed exclusively by Rosen Publishing.

To see additional Britannica Educational Publishing titles, go to rosenpublishing.com.

First Edition

<u>Britannica Educational Publishing</u>
J.E. Luebering: Director, Core Reference Group
Mary Rose McCudden: Editor, Britannica Student Encyclopedia

<u>Rosen Publishing</u>
Hope Lourie Killcoyne: Executive Editor
Tracey Baptiste: Editor
Nelson Sá: Art Director
Nicole Russo: Designer
Cindy Reiman: Photography Manager

Library of Congress Cataloging-in-Publication Data

Cummings, Matthew.
What is the legislative branch?/Matthew Cummings. — First edition.
        pages cm. — Let's find out! Government)
Includes bibliographical references and index.
ISBN 978-1-62275-956-9 (library bound) — ISBN 978-1-62275-957-6 (pbk.) — ISBN 978-1-62275-959-0 (6-pack)
1. United States. Congress—Juvenile literature. I. Title.
JK1025.C85 2015
328.73—dc23

                                                                          2014038507

Manufactured in the United States of America

Photo credits: Cover, interior pages background image Vlad G/Shutterstock.com; p. 4 Chip Somodevilla/Getty Images News/Thinkstock; p. 5 Orhan Cam/Shutterstock.com; pp. 6, 13 Official White House Photo by David Lienemann; p. 7 NARA; pp. 8, 29 Library of Congress Prints and Photographs Division; p. 9 Architect of the Capitol; p. 11 Douglas Graham/CQ-Roll Call Group/Getty Images; p. 12 Win McNamee/Getty Images; p. 14 Mark Wilson/Getty Images News/Thinkstock; p. 15 Alex Wong/Getty Images News/Thinkstock; p. 16 nazlisart/Shutterstock.com; p. 17 Bill Clark/CQ-Roll Call Group/Getty Images; p. 18 Official White House Photo by Pete Souza; p. 19 Steve Petteway, Collection of the Supreme Court of the United States; p. 20 Marine Corps photo by Lance Cpl. Sullivan Laramie; p. 21 U.S. Air Force photo; p. 22 Spencer Platt/Getty Images; p. 23 Alexander Raths/Shutterstock.com; p. 24 Adam Parent/Shutterstock.com; p. 25 © iStockphoto.com/Alina555; p. 26 AlexKol Photography/Shutterstock.com; p. 27 Lassie Kristensen/Shutterstock.com; p. 28 © iStockphoto.com/GeorgePeters

CONTENTS

WHAT IS THE LEGISLATIVE BRANCH?

There are three parts, also called branches, of the U.S. government. One of them is the legislative branch. It makes laws, and it can declare war. It can also approve or disapprove of the people that a president might want for a government job, like Supreme Court judge.

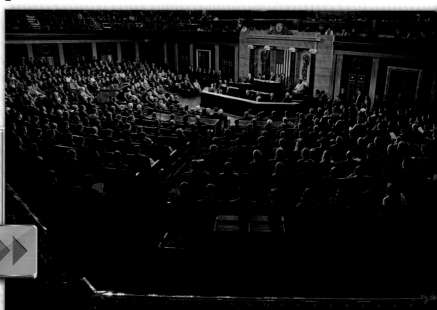

Members of the U.S. Congress meet at the U.S. Capitol in Washington, D.C.

The U.S. Capitol houses the U.S. Congress. It is also used for special ceremonies, such as presidential inaugurations.

The legislative branch is also called Congress. Congress is made up of two houses or groups: the Senate and the House of Representatives, or the House. The Senate and the House both meet at the U.S. Capitol, a building located in Washington, D.C. Congress has the power to make laws that allow the government to do its job of serving the American people.

The United States government gets its powers from the United States Constitution. The Constitution is a document that explains how the government should work. It also lists the rights of the people of the country.

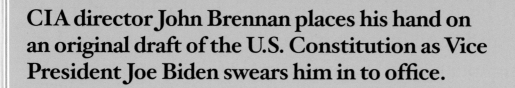

CIA director John Brennan places his hand on an original draft of the U.S. Constitution as Vice President Joe Biden swears him in to office.

The other two branches of the government are the executive branch and the judicial branch. The Constitution gives each branch separate powers. The executive branch enforces the laws that the legislative branch makes. The president is the head of the executive branch. The judicial branch includes the Supreme Court and other courts. All three branches of government check each other to make sure no one branch uses more power than it should.

In 1789, the Constitution was signed and put into effect. This action created an official government for the United States with a set of rules they would use to govern the country.

The original Constitution can be viewed at the National Archives in Washington, D.C.

THINK ABOUT IT
The United States has the oldest written constitution. Why is a constitution important to a country?

The U.S. Constitution is the oldest written constitution still in use.

How the Legislature Was Formed

In 1781, the 13 American colonies won their independence from Great Britain. They established a new government and became states rather than colonies. The new government did not work well, however. In 1787, representatives from each of the states met in Philadelphia, Pennsylvania, to solve the problems. At the convention, they wrote the new Constitution. When they discussed

This piece of art, in the archives of the Library of Congress, depicts George Washington during the Revolutionary War.

WASHINGTON, CROSSING THE DELAWARE.

On the Evening of Dec. 25th 1776, previous to the battle of Trenton.

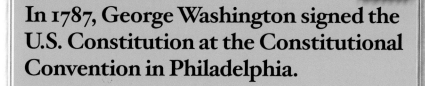

In 1787, George Washington signed the U.S. Constitution at the Constitutional Convention in Philadelphia.

the legislative branch, each state had its own concerns. Each state wanted a way for its concerns to be addressed. Larger states had different issues than smaller ones. The smaller states wanted to be sure they had as much of a voice as the larger states. All of the states agreed to a system with two houses. Each house would have representatives from all thirteen states. These representatives could speak for each state's people.

MEMBERS OF CONGRESS

The two houses of Congress have several differences. In the Senate there are 100 senators, two from each state. Senators serve six-year terms. A term is the length of time a person holds an office. The people of each state elect their senators.

The House is made up of 435 representatives. States with bigger populations have more representatives than states with smaller populations. States that have more than one representative are divided into sections. These sections are called districts. People

Today, you can learn about your senators and representatives representatives by visiting many different Internet websites.

Each new class of Congress is photographed on the steps of the U.S. Capitol Building.

THINK ABOUT IT

Each of the three branches of the U.S. government has a limited amount of power. Why is this important?

vote only for the representative from the district in which they live. They cannot vote for representatives from other districts. Representatives serve two-year terms.

The Constitution requires that a census is taken every ten years. A census gathers basic information, including how many people live in each state. That number is used to decide how many representatives each state should have.

Congressional Leadership

Both the Senate and House of Representatives have leaders. The House leader is called the speaker of the House. The political party that has the most members in the House is called the majority party. Members of that party get to vote for the speaker. The speaker's job is to oversee the meetings of the House.

VOCABULARY

A **political party** is a group of people who usually have similar beliefs about the role of government and how it should be run.

John Boehner became the speaker of the House of Representatives in 2011.

The vice president is the leader of the U.S. Senate. The vice president under Barack Obama was Joe Biden.

The Senate leader is called the president of the Senate. The vice president of the United States serves as president of the Senate. However, the vice president votes only if there is a tie. Another senator, called the president pro tempore, leads the Senate when the vice president is absent. The president pro tempore is one of the senators. The majority party in the Senate votes for the president pro tempore.

The minority party, or the party with the fewest members in each house, also has a leader. This person is called the Senate minority leader or the House minority

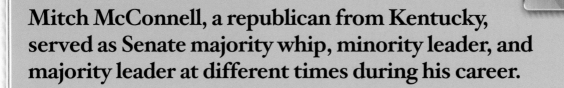

Mitch McConnell, a republican from Kentucky, served as Senate majority whip, minority leader, and majority leader at different times during his career.

leader. This person speaks for his or her party and helps to decide what kind of projects or laws the party is going to work on. The minority leader may also be called the leader of the opposition. It is his or her job to make sure the ideas of the minority party are heard.

Senator Richard Durbin, a democrat from Illinois, served as the Senate majority whip for ten years. He became the minority whip when the Republicans gained control of the Senate in 2015.

Both parties also have whips. A whip is the person who manages the members of each party. Whips make sure party members show up when there is a vote. They also work to make sure members vote on issues important to their party.

COMPARE AND CONTRAST

There are two major political parties in the United States: the Democrats and the Republicans. Each has its own set of ideals. Why is this good for government?

LEGISLATIVE POWERS: CREATING LAWS

1. A bill is proposed.

2. The bill is debated.

3. The bill is approved OR the bill is vetoed.

A bill goes through many steps before it becomes a law.

The legislative branch creates laws. A new law starts out as a document called a bill.

For a bill to become a law, a member of the House or Senate has to introduce it. Then the bill goes to committee. This is a small group of senators or representatives who review the bill. Once the bill is ready, it is sent to the full House or Senate. House and Senate members debate, or talk, about the bill. Then they vote to pass or reject the bill. If more than half of each house's members approve the bill, it then goes to the other house for a vote. In order to become a law, both houses must pass a bill.

Members of Congress can ask questions when a bill is presented for a vote.

THINK ABOUT IT

Why is it necessary to have so many steps to create a law?

Once a bill is passed it goes to the president of the United States. If the president signs the bill, it becomes

The president of the United States is the only person who can sign a bill into a law. He can also veto, or reject, a bill.

a law. The president can veto, or reject, a bill. A vetoed bill can still become a law, however. This happens if two-thirds of both houses vote to override, or undo, the veto.

If people think there is a problem with a law they may ask the Supreme Court to review the law. The Supreme Court is the highest court in the country.

Sandra Day O'Connor (far left) was the first woman on the Supreme Court. Other women justices include Sonia Sotomayor, Ruth Bader Ginsburg, and Elena Kagan.

Vocabulary

To **violate** means to break or fail to observe a rule.

The court may decide that the law violates the U.S. Constitution. In that case, the law is no longer in force. This makes sure Congress doesn't create laws that are not in the best interest of the people, and it protects people's rights.

LEGISLATIVE POWERS: DECLARING WAR

Congress has the ability to declare war, when it is necessary for our country to defend itself or its people. This power is sometimes called the War Powers Clause.

For Congress to declare war, the president must ask Congress to vote on whether the government should or should not declare war on

Congress alone can decide if the United States should declare war on another nation.

The U.S. military continuously trains for action at home and around the world.

another country. Two-thirds of both the Senate and the House must vote in favor of declaring war. That means 66 members of the Senate and 287 members of the House must vote yes.

But not all military actions need the official approval of Congress. The president can send troops to handle different situations that require the military if it is necessary. These are not considered acts of war.

THINK ABOUT IT

Congress has formally declared war on only five occasions: the War of 1812, the Mexican-American War, the Spanish-American War, World War I, and World War II. Why have so few wars been declared?

Legislative Powers: Taxes and Money

Congress can create and collect taxes. The money collected from taxes is used to help the United States in many ways.

Taxes are used for construction projects on roads and public buildings. Social programs like medical care, education, and Social Security are also supported

Every year people must send the government forms to show that they have paid their taxes. They can mail the forms or send them through the Internet.

The federal government supports a wide range of services to the American people, including health care programs for the elderly and poor.

by taxes. Tax money is also used to support the men and women who serve in the military. It is used to buy equipment and weapons for the troops. Taxes are also used to help run the national parks and programs in the arts.

Sometimes the government collects less money than it needs to operate all of its programs and services. The government is allowed to borrow money to make up the difference.

THINK ABOUT IT

Every citizen and business has to pay taxes to the government. Why do you think this is important?

Congress is able to tell the U.S. Treasury to issue bonds. Bonds are basically loans between the government and the people who buy them. When people buy bonds, the government gets the money. The money must be paid back by a certain date. Some of the taxes that the government collects are used to pay back the money for the bonds. Congress decides how the money from the bonds is spent. Congress cannot raise money this way all the time. There is a limit to how much debt the government can have.

Congress created the Federal Reserve System to provide financial services—like a bank—to the

The Federal Reserve makes sure that banks have enough money to lend to people and to cash checks.

THINK ABOUT IT
The Elastic Clause is power granted to Congress to make any laws they feel are "necessary and proper" for carrying out its duties. How is this helpful?

U.S. government. It makes sure that the economy of the country is healthy. It also makes sure that money moves through the banking system smoothly. For example, it makes sure that payments, such as paychecks, are made properly.

Legislative Powers: Regulating Trade

The Constitution grants Congress the power to regulate trade with other countries. Trade is an exchange of goods or services. Congress manages trade by deciding on what can and cannot come into the United

Cargo ships import and export goods around the world. Congress regulates this type of trade.

Congress may tax imported goods in order to make goods created in the United States easier to buy.

States. They can also put taxes on imports—the goods that are brought in. The taxes may make the goods more expensive to buy than American-made products. This may make it more likely that people will buy American-made products instead of ones from other countries. The government may also stop trading with another country for economic or political reasons. For example, Congress may not want to trade with a country whose government is doing something that the United States disagrees with.

THINK ABOUT IT
What kind of goods might be traded with other countries?

LEGISLATIVE POWERS: OTHER POWERS

In addition to making laws, Congress has a lot of other powers. It can coin, or make, money. It provides patents and copyrights for new ideas. A patent or copyright makes sure that a person or business cannot steal an idea from another person or business.

Congress manages the United States post office. For example, it can set how many days of the week

Coining money is another job of Congress.

mail is delivered. Congress also sets the rules for people who want to become U.S. citizens.

Another power Congress has is the ability to impeach the president or other officials. It does this if it thinks the official has broken the law. First, the House of Representatives impeaches, or brings charges against, an official. The Senate then holds a trial and acts as the judge. If the Senate finds the official guilty, the official must leave his or her job.

ANDREW JOHNSON.

Congress can impeach the president of the United States. In 1868, Andrew Johnson became the first president to be impeached.

GLOSSARY

colonies Counties or areas under the control of another country.

committee A smaller group that works in support of a larger group.

debate To discuss an issue to understand both sides.

delegates People with the power to act for another person or group; representatives.

district An area of land overseen by a local government.

document A written representation of one's thoughts or ideas.

employees People who work for a salary.

federal Relating to the national level of government.

financial Having to do with money.

govern To rule over.

import To bring goods into a country from someplace else for sale.

judicial Relating to the court system.

majority More than half of the total.

military The armed forces, including the army, air force, navy, and marines.

minority Less than half of the total.

misconduct Unacceptable behavior.

patent A legal protection to someone who has an idea or invention.

regulate To adjust the amount, rate, or speed of something.

term A fixed or limited period of time.

veto To reject a decision made by a law-making body.

FOR MORE INFORMATION

Jakubiak, David J. *What Does a Congressional Representative Do?* New York, NY: Rosen Publishing, 2010.

Jakubiak, David J. *What Does a Senator Do?* New York, NY: Rosen Publishing, 2010.

Nelson, Robin, and Sandy Donoval. *The Congress: A Look at the Legislative Branch.* Minneapolis, MN: Lerner Publications, 2012.

Nichols, Clive. *Taxes and Government Spending.* New York, NY: Rosen Publishing, 2012.

Sobel, Syl. *How the U.S. Government Works.* Hauppauge, NY: Barron's Educational Series, 2012.

Taylor-Butler, Christine. *The Congress of the United States.* New York, NY: Scholastic, 2008.

Websites

Because of the changing nature of Internet links, Rosen Publishing has developed an online list of websites related to the subject of this book. This site is updated regularly. Please use this link to access the list:

http://www.rosenlinks.com/LFO/Legis

Index